SUPERBASE 25

PAX RIVER

SUPERBASE 25

PAX RIVER

Naval Air Test Center

T. Malcolm English

OSPREY
AEROSPACE

Acknowledgements

Space precludes individual acknowledgement for all of the assistance given to the author in preparing this book particularly by the many personnel at Pax River who devoted their time to answering endless questions. However, the author would like to express particular gratitude to Rear Admiral Donald V Boecker, officer commanding the Naval Air Test Center, for approving my visit to the NATC; Lola Hilton and John Romer of the Public Affairs Office for their help and hospitality; and the Pax River photographic section for permission to use the excellent air-to-air photographs contained in this book. The author must also thank Ian Dickens, General Manager – Consumer Division of Olympus Optical Co (UK) Ltd, for the loan of equipment. With the exception of the air-to-air photographs, all of the photographs in this book were taken with Olympus cameras.

Published in 1992 by Osprey Publishing Limited, 59 Grosvenor Street, London W1X 9DA

© T Malcolm English 1992

ISBN 1 85532 215 3

Editor Tony Holmes
Page design by Paul Kime
Printed in Hong Kong

For Aileen, without whose patience and understanding this book would not have been possible

Front cover The A-6 Intruder has an enviable record as a strike aircraft of devastating potency, and who could argue the point after studying this remarkable photograph. Loaded up with over a dozen Mk 82 500 lb retarded Snakeye bombs, this Intruder from the Strike Test Directorate is conducting an evaluation sortie to examine the handling of an A-6 fully armed up. With each of its five stores pylons stressed for loads of up to 3600 lbs, the Intruder can carry no less than 18,000 lbs of ordnance, although more typically it would carry a mix of bombs and external fuel tanks (*US Navy photo*)

Back cover The subject of a much protracted development programme, the McDonell Douglas T-45A Goshawk is finally nearing clearance for squadron service with the US Navy's many training units. Based on the highly successful British Aerospace Hawk, the T-45 has suffered from extensive weight growth as McDonnell Douglas strived to make the aircraft suitable for carrier operations. To compensate for this, the Goshawk has been fitted with the more powerful Rolls-Royce Turboméca Adour 871 turbofan

Title page Built as an F-14A, Grumman's development Tomcat, BuNo 162595 (Modex 221), is currently operated by the Strike Aircraft Test Directorate (Strike) and has been equipped with a number of D model systems. These include the General Electric Aerospace Electronic Systems infra-red search and track sensor, protected whilst on the ground by a lens cover

Right Ling Temco Vought A-7E Corsair II (BuNo 160565) with arrestor hook lowered for a simulated carrier deck landing and arrestor wire engagement. Strike operates a ground-based TC-7 arresting gear to test an aircraft's carrier suitability under controlled conditions

---

For a catalogue of all books published by Osprey Aerospace please write to:

The Marketing Department, Octopus Illustrated Books, 1st Floor, Michelin House, 81 Fulham Road, London SW3 6RB

Introduction

Naval Air Station Patuxent River, or Pax River as it is familiarly known, has been the focal point of US Naval flight testing since its commissioning in 1943. Prior to World War 2, the US Navy flight test facilities were widely dispersed throughout the United States. They are now co-located at the Naval Air Test Center (NATC), to test and evaluate integrated naval air weapon systems throughout their life-cycle.

Situated at the mouth of the Patuxent River, the station occupies approximately 6400 acres overlooking the picturesque Chesapeake Bay, in an area the *New York Times* once called 'Maryland's buried treasure'. Pax River is more than just an airfield – some 5500 acres of the station are open to recreational activities, such as hunting, boating and hiking. It also has a golf course which is sanctioned by the PGA.

Out of the total of 12,000 personnel at Pax River, approximately 6700 are employed by the NATC, the remainder by the 50 tenant units on the station. The vast majority of the funding for the NATC ($350 million per year) is provided by Naval Air Systems Command. Additional income is provided by its other customers, such as the USAF, NASA and FAA.

About 140 aircraft are operated by NATC, representing all of the types currently in operational service with the US Navy, and many outside the inventory. Six directorates evaluate specific segments of naval aviation:-

Strike Aircraft Test Directorate: is responsible for testing experimental and production fixed wing attack, fighter and other specifically designated aircraft, including V/STOL. Approximately 60 aircraft, comprising seven different types, are flown by Strike.

Rotary Wing Aircraft Test Directorate: as its name implies, this is the US Navy's primary organization for testing Navy and Marine Corps helicopter and tilt rotor aircraft and their mission equipment.

Force Warfare Aircraft Test Directorate: participates in the complete spectrum of life cycle phases for all types of fixed wing aircraft in the US Navy inventory and leads field activities on airborne early warning. It has three major programme areas to manage a variety of departments including administration, lighter than air projects and aircraft maintenance.

Systems Engineering Test Directorate: undertakes the task of simulating mission environments and evaluating all systems within US Navy aircraft, such as computers, ejection seats, electrical systems and electronic warfare systems. It is particularly proud of its Air Combat Environmental Test and Evaluation Facility, which combines several laboratories and man-in-the-loop simulator to replicate actual flight conditions in a wide variety of environments.

Range Directorate: supports flight testing by providing expertise for instrumenting aircraft and capturing data from flight tests. Six aircraft can be monitored simultaneously, each generating up to 2000 independent data measurements. This directorate is also responsible for maintaining a variety of fixed and mobile targets.

Computer Sciences Directorate: takes flight test data and processes it, as well as providing computer support for a vast range of activities on the station.

Arguably the best known unit at Pax River is the US Navy Test Pilot School (TPS). As part of the NATC, the school provides the Test Center and the rest of the research, development, test and evaluation community with the test pilots, test flight officers and test project engineers needed for the continued development and improvement of the US Navy's fleet assets.

Competition for places in the school is fierce and most aircrew are required to have a minimum of 1500 hours to qualify for acceptance. Two courses, each having some 34 students, are run concurrently in three disciplines; fixed wing, rotary wing and systems. Many famous pilots are numbered among the graduates of the TPS including Alan Shepard, who became the first American in space and Rear Admiral Donald V Boecker, commander of the NATC.

During the commissioning ceremony, almost half a century ago, the late Rear Admiral John S McCain, then chief of the US Navy's Bureau of Aeronautics, called Pax River 'the most needed station in the Navy'. Paradoxically, for a station breaking through the frontiers of technology, it can be said 'there ain't nothing new' – it still is.

(*Author's note*: The Naval Air Test Center was renamed the Naval Air Warfare Center, Aircraft Division as of 1st January 1991.)

Contents

Above A pilot and his bombardier-navigator from Strike walk back to the crew-room for a debrief following a weapons dispersion sortie in a Grumman A-6E Intruder

Tomcats and Hornets

Left Strike's aircrew have the unique and envious opportunity of flying the most potent combat aircraft in the West, if not the world. Included in their fleet are examples of the McDonnell Douglas F/A-18 Hornet and F-14A Tomcat

Below Paradoxically, the low-visibility markings of this F-14D, the third of its type to be built, make it stand-out amongst the more gaudily coloured aircraft on Strike's ramp. Externally, the Delta is almost identical to the Alpha variant, the most obvious difference being the former's two chin-pods which house the infra-red search and track and television set camera. Internally, it has been equipped with a Hughes APG-71 radar and Mil-Std 1553 data bus. One of the many benefits associated with the fitment of the General Electric F110-GE-400 engines is that it allows carrier take-offs in military (dry) power. Pratt & Whitney TF30-P-414A powered F-14As normally use re-heat for catapult shots

McDonnell Douglas T-45A Goshawk and its A-7E Corsair II chase aircraft hold for take-off whilst an F-14A lands. All of these aircraft are in Strike's inventory, illustrating its commitment to evaluate production and new aircraft types

Above Dayglow orange fin and unit crest identify this F-14 as one of the 60 aircraft on the strength of Strike

Left Flight data such as airspeed, aircraft attitude and position, is transmitted in real-time to the Test Center by Tactical Airborne Combat Telemetry System (TACTS) pods, carried by trials aircraft such as this F-14

Above Mission capability and survivability of current generation tactical aircraft, such as this Hughes AIM-54 Phoenix-armed F-14 Tomcat, are enhanced by complex avionics systems. However, it is essential that compatibility of these diverse systems is achieved before the aircraft enters service. Individual systems may operate as designed, but when integrated into a full-up weapons platform, mutual interference may degrade performance. This Aircraft Anechoic Test Facility (AATF) provides a vital link to full operational clearance, complementing the flight trials programme and thus reducing the number of costly and sometimes hazardous flights (*US Navy photo*)

Left Aircraft size can be deceptive, particularly that of fighters. This pilot from Strike, carrying out a pre-flight inspection of an F-14, lends scale to the aircraft

Above left Considering that he had just landed from a sortie in which his F-14 Tomcat had 'trounced' an F/A-18 Hornet in air-combat, Lt Cdr Lee 'Mortis' Graham is looking particularly 'cool'. Lt Cdr Graham is Executive Assistant of the Strike Aircraft Test Directorate

Above right Cdr George 'Luke' Luechauer, the T-45TS Project Officer at Strike. He is also a mean air-combat pilot having just flown an extremely successful Tomcat sortie with 'Mortis' Graham, against an F/A-18

Left This view emphasizes the Hornet's distinctive leading edge extension, an aerodynamic feature designed to enable the wing to operate at a higher angle of attack. It also straightens the airflow into the engine air-intakes at these high angles. That it did so, to the US Navy's satisfaction, was for Strike to determine

Overleaf Laden with instrumentation and eight 1000 lb bombs, F/A-18B, BuNo 161497 rolls for take-off. The tailplane trim angle is clearly set for climb-out on this Hornet

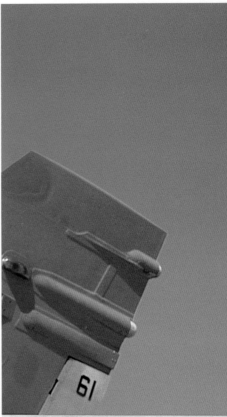

Above Photographed from the Hornet's cockpit by a helpful technician, a total of eight Mk 83 low-drag 1000 lb general purpose bombs are loaded for jettison trials. Demonstrating safe weapon separation is one of Strike's primary tasks. The bombs' blue colour-code scheme indicates that they are inert stores

Right Weapon jettison trials are filmed by a battery of strategically placed cameras, such as this pair mounted on the F/A-18's wing-tip

Because of the increasing dependence on avionics for aircraft stability and
weapons system operation, avionic studies are an important element of the Test
Pilot School (TPS) syllabus, with laboratory demonstrations and classroom
'chalk and talk' being backed up by practical demonstrations in the School's
aircraft. F/A-18B Hornet '01' (BuNo 161249) is admirably suited for the task,
having a fly-by-wire system, and probably one of the most advanced avionics
data-display installations of any military aircraft currently in service

This pristine F/A-18D is one of Strike's latest acquisitions. Like its F/A-18C single-seat equivalent, the 'D' variant has provision for carrying up to six Hughes AIM-120 AMRAAMs and four imaging infra-red AGM-65F Mavericks. Other systems improvements to the F/A-18A/B standard aircraft include improved mission computers, an internal AN/ALQ-165 airborne self-protection jammer and Martin Baker NACES ejection seats

Above Ground support for Strike's flight trials is provided by an amalgam of civilian, Navy and Marine Corps personnel. Marine Corps technicians are primarily employed in servicing and maintaining the Directorate's Hornets and Harrier IIs. Dressed to match Strike's high visibility colour schemes, a technician obliges the author by taking a photograph of bombs being loaded

Left In its operational air-defence role the F/A-18A Hornet's normal missile configuration is two wing-tip mounted AIM-9L Sidewinders and four AIM-7F Sparrows, two mounted on the outboard underwing stations and two on the lower sides of the fuselage air-inlets. A87 is flight testing a dual launcher installation on the port under-wing pylon, which would allow two AIM-120 AMRAAMs to be carried on each pylon

Above Aircraft tested in the AATF are suspended from the chamber crane using a fabric sling to prevent disturbing the electromagnetic field. There is unlikely to be a 'sudden-twang' as the crane's 60,000 lbs lifting capacity is more than double the weight of this Royal Australian Air Force F/A-18B Hornet. The Hornet is equipped with Martin Marietta AN/ASQ-173 laser spot tracker/strike camera and Ford AN/AAS-38 Forward Looking Infra-red (FLIR) pods on the fuselage cheek stations (*US Navy photo*)

Left Note the angled wing-tip launcher rails for the AIM-9L Sidewinder on this F/A-18D Hornet. Other test centres, such as China Lake and Point Mugu, evaluate armament performance, but only Pax River tests aircraft as a fully integrated weapon system

Salty veterans

Above One of Strike's workhorses is this A-4M Skyhawk (BuNo 158430) with airbrakes open for landing. The blisters aside the nose and above the engine jet-pipe and the fin-tip pod, contain antennae for the electronic counter measure (ECM). The orange coloured probe below the nose is an electronic surveillance measure (ESM) aerial

Right An A-4M Skyhawk is guided down the glideslope by the Fresnel lens optical landing system. Developed for carrier-deck landings, the system provides a stable reference for the pilot

Above Six A-4Ms on Strike's flightline. It is over 37 years since the prototype XA4D-1 first flew, this much later version having experienced middle age weight growth. However, unlike pilots suffering the same complaint, its performance has actually increased. Between the initial A-4A variant, as the XA4D-1 was redesignated, and the A-4M, maximum take-off weight has increased by some 22 per cent and external weapons load by 83 per cent. Thus, weapon load has increased to over 37 per cent of maximum take-off weight, compared with the A-4A's's 25 per cent

Right The Skyhawk's distinctive nose undercarriage is typical of the design features adopted by its designer Ed Heinemann to save weight and minimize complexity. It is configured to retract forward below the cockpit so that the emergency lowering is assisted by both gravity and aerodynamic drag. In all respects, the Skyhawk conforms to Heinemann's oft quoted acronym 'KISS' (Keep It Simple Stupid). As this TA-4J of the TPS, and other two-seater variants, were intended purely for advanced flying training, additional weight savings were possible by deleting much of the nav-attack system

Right A rather weather-beaten TPS TA-4J, framed by the jet-pipe of one of its more immaculate stablemates. Having a less demanding performance requirement than the single-seat variant, the 'standard' TA-4J is fitted with an engine of lower thrust; the Pratt & Whitney J52-P-6 (8500 lbs st). It does, however, have the provision for fitting a P & W J52-P-8A (9300 lbs st)

Above TA-4J BuNo 158118 in the distinctive dayglo orange and white training unit colours, on a visit from the recently retired training carrier USS *Lexington* (CTW-1)

Above An OA-4M of Strike on finals to land

Left Of all the aircraft types in the TPS inventory, the Skyhawk must surely be a classic example of excellence achieved by application of sound aerodynamic and engineering principles to aircraft design

Above With its square tipped fin and nose and tail antennae, the OA-4M bears a marked resemblance to the A-4M; in fact, the OA-4M fleet first saw life as TA-4Fs. A total of 23 TA-4Fs were converted to OA-4Ms for the US Marine Corps, their primary role being forward air control for Navy and Marine attack aircraft

Above right After an initial lack of interest by the US Navy in a two-seat trainer version of the Corsair II, 60 A-7B and A-7C models were converted and designated TA-7C. The dayglo orange aircraft (BuNo 154477) was the prototype conversion and flew for the first time in December 1976. Both aircraft are carrying data transmitter pods, which send real-time information to the Test Center for Strike (*US Navy photo*)

Right Although the Corsair II's folding wings were a requirement dictated by carrier operations, it is an equally useful feature when taxying and parking at land bases

Above Captain Raymond A Dudderar, preflights a TA-7C Corsair II before a departing on a sortie from the NATC, where he is director of the Strike Aircraft Test Directorate. Dudderar, who had been chief test pilot for Strike, became its director in April 1989

Right Strike's Corsair IIs sport a variety of colour schemes, from the early gull-grey and white, with and without dayglo orange panels, to low-visibility grey

Sub-hunters and spin-offs

Left Viking colours; a gull-grey Viking S-3B, framed by the nose of the ES-3A in high visibility dayglo markings, provides a stark contrast of colour schemes on the Force Warfare Test Directorate (Force) flightline

Below 'Hurry-up, I can't hold this all day.' Engineers of Force at work on a buddy-buddy refuelling pod for an S-3 Viking. In its tanker role, the Viking carries a standard 300 US gal (1136 litre) fuel tank under the starboard wing and a pod, containing drogue and hose, under the port wing

Left In-flight refuelling can justifiably claim to be a force (no pun intended) multiplier by extending combat air patrol times and extending the range of strike aircraft, hence the interest in developing in-flight refuelling technology and techniques. The Viking was an unsuccessful candidate for the dedicated air-to-air refuelling tanker role (only one aircraft was ever modified to KS-3A specs) when fitted with an integral hose drum unit and extra fuel tanks in the weapons bay

Above Large, curved windscreen panels afford an excellent field of view for the pilot and co-pilot who, together with the sensor operator and tactical co-ordinator, sit in Douglas Escapac ejection seats. Although the Viking relies heavily on electronic sensors to detect targets, the 'mark one' eye-ball is still an important asset

Above left Fin markings of aircraft on the strength of Air Test and Evaluation Squadron ONE (VX-1), such as this S-3 Viking, clearly indicate the squadron's anti-submarine warfare (ASW) role

Above right VX-1 originated in April 1943 with the commissioning of the Air Anti-submarine Development Detachment. It adopted its present title in 1969 and over the years has diversified into a number of projects not directly related to ASW. An example of this is the operational testing of the Grumman EA-6A Intruder. Aircraft currently undergoing development with VX-1 include the Lockheed P-3 and EP-3 Orion, S-3A/B Viking Sikorsky, SH-3H Sea King SH-60B Seahawk and Kaman Seasprite

Left Tactics developed by VX-1 to locate submerged submarines include the use of magnetic anomaly detectors (MAD). The S-3 Viking's retractable Texas Instruments AN/ASQ-81 MAD boom is seen here in the extended position

Above Demonstrating the Viking's operational flexibility, an S-3B fires a salvo of unguided rockets from underwing pods. This test typifies the work done by Force to expand the role of the Navy's fixed-wing fleet (*US Navy photo*)

Left The Lockheed ES-3A is an electronic reconnaissance variant of the S-3A Viking anti-submarine aircraft, and is intended to provide carrier battle groups with their own intelligence gathering capability. This particular aircraft, BuNo 157993, is the second Viking produced and has been fitted with aerodynamically representative fairings, radomes and antennae for flying qualities testing

In addition to the distinctive dorsal fairing and three large radomes, the ES-3A sports no fewer than 35 antennae, all of which are electronically inert. A long instrumented nose boom, which was fitted for flight tests, was removed when the programme was cancelled, prior to the aircraft being shipped to NAS Cecil Field, Florida, for permanent display

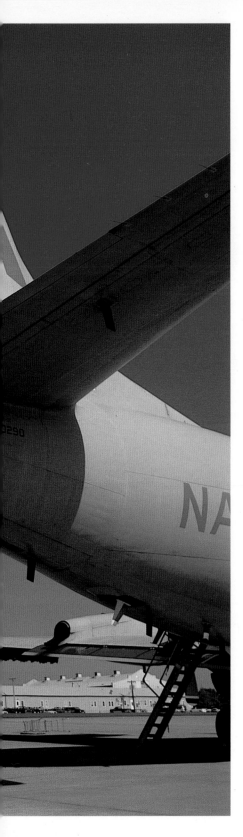

Left One of the primary tasks of Force is to ensure that the US Navy retains its lead in ASW technology. To this end, its three patrol aviation test laboratories are performing studies to develop a replacement for the Lockheed P-3 Orion. In addition, Force has three P-3B and three P-3C models for development flying trials

Above 'Open wide'; the nose cone of a P-3C is lifted to expose the APS-115 radar set for maintenance. As part of an ongoing improvement programme, the P-3C Orion is now receiving Update 4 equipment, such as GPS (Global Positioning System), upgraded electronic support measures equipment and the APS-137 radar

Above A tow bar provides a convenient 'perch' for two ground crew of the Naval Research Laboratory (NRL) Flight Support Detachment, while they hold open the undercarriage door of a P-3A. In the background is a UP-3A, BuNo 150607. The NRL Flight Support Detachment provides operationally ready aircraft and trained flight crews in direct support of the NRL airborne research projects. The detachment maintains and operates four P-3 variants, with 60 military and five civilian personnel assigned

Right Technicians at work on one of the 4910 shp Allison T56 turboprop engines, which power Force's P-3C Orions

Above *Project Outpost Seascan* is one of three projects assigned to the RP-3Ds of VXN-8. This mission calls for world-wide oceanographic data observation and surveys. The information gathered is used for operational fleet support and generating a data base for the prediction of the US Navy's anti-submarine warfare environment

Right Of the three Lockheed RP-3Ds on the strength of Oceanographic Development Squadron EIGHT (VXN-8), that tasked with *Project Magnet* carries the greatest load of scientific equipment

Left VXN-8 is the West's only aviation squadron devoted solely to airborne oceanographic and geomagnetic surveys. The squadron is a fleet command under the administrative control of Commander Patrol Wings, Atlantic and the operational control of Commander in Chief, US Atlantic Fleet. As such, VXN-8 functions as a separate fleet command, but receives technical direction from the Navy Oceanographic Office (NAVOCEANO). The three projects currently assigned to the squadron are *Project Birdseye*, *Magnet* and *Outpost Seascan*

Top Choice of 'El Coyote' for the designation of VXN-8's *Project Outpost Seascan* RP-3D reflects its missions in remote regions, far removed from heavily occupied sea-lanes. For *Outpost Seascan* sorties the RP-3D is manned by a four to six-man team of NAVOCEANO scientists and technicians and a twelve-man crew from VXN-8. *Outpost Seascan* instrumentation has been updated to provide the same capabilities for collecting Arctic environmental data as the *Project Birdseye* aircraft

Above As its name implies, *Project Magnet* involves the collection of accurate and current world-wide geomagnetic data. Established in 1951, it is the oldest of VXN-8's three projects, the information obtained being used in the construction of magnetic, nautical, aeronautical and military charts. The 'Roadrunner' designation symbolizes the project's need for speedy dissemination of up-to-date information

Above Based on the Army's UH-60A Black Hawk, the Seahawk embodies a number of changes to integrate the mission equipment and to provide shipboard compatibility. One such change is the addition of the Texas Instruments AN/ASQ-81(V)2 MAD equipment, the brightly coloured MAD 'bird' being carried on the starboard fuselage side

Right One of the latest aircraft to be evaluated by VX-1 is the Sikorsky SH-60B LAMPS III Seahawk. Indeed, the LAMPS (Light Airborne Multi-purpose System) III weapon system has completed one of the most successful research, development, test and evaluation programmes in modern weapon procurement history

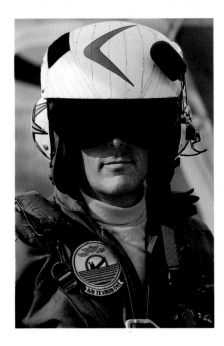

Above Commander Randy Abshier, the commanding officer of VX-1, photographed after an evaluation flight in the squadron's SH-60B. Commander Abshier has two Mediterranean deployments to his credit aboard the aircraft carriers USS *Saratoga* (CV-60) and USS John F Kennedy (CV-67). Before taking command of the Pax River unit in 1989, he was executive officer aboard USS *Guam* (LPH-9)

Right The Mk 50 Advanced Lightweight Torpedo (ALWT) is just one of the many weapons evaluated by VX-1. Having similar dimensions to its predecessor, the Mk 46 ALWT is designed to have a larger target detection envelope and capabilities against both deep diving submarines and surface ships. A feasibility study, carried out in 1990 to investigate the carriage of four ALWTs in the weapons bay of the S-3 Viking, highlighted significant structural clearance problems to be resolved

Left With open doors looking like a large pair of 'ears', the SH-60B's real 'ears' are its sensor suite comprising sonobuoys, MAD, search radar and electronic support measures. Usually powered by two General Electric CT7 turboshaft engines, the Seahawk has also been tested at VX-1 with two 2100 shp (shaft horsepower) Rolls-Royce/Turbomeca RTM 522 fitted in place of the CT7s

Above An SH-60F Ocean Hawk in the AATF undergoing compatibility trials of its Allied Signal AN/AQS-13F dipping sonar system. Developed from the SH-60B, the Ocean Hawk is intended to operate from aircraft carriers and provide protection against submarine attack for the inner zone of a carrier battle group. Much of the SH-60B's systems have been removed, including the prominent nose-mounted ESM fairings (*US Navy photo*)

Above One of the six Sikorsky SH-3D Sea Kings on the strength of Pax River's
search and rescue (SAR) helicopter unit. The unit is nicknamed 'The SAR Dogs'
due to its aggressive attitude in achieving mission objectives

Right Unlike emergency scrambles, training sorties allow for relatively
leisurely pre-flight checks of the SAR unit's SH-3D Sea King

Above Lt Brad Hartung, a Search and Rescue pilot with the 'Pax River SAR Dogs' unit

Left An uncharacteristically coloured SAR Sea King. Most SAR aircraft, operating in peacetime have high visibility dayglo markings to aid sighting and identification

Strike!

Right One of the less aerodynamic weapons in the US Navy inventory is the Mk 60 mine. Otherwise known as CAPTOR, a contraction of 'encapsulated torpedo', it comprises a Mk 46 torpedo inserted into a mine casing. Note the slight yaw angle of the mines as they fall away from the underwing stations of this A-6E TRAM of Strike (*US Navy photo*)

Above An A-6E TRAM Intruder, armed with Mk 82 Snakeye retarded bombs, wheels over storm clouds. TRAM (target-recognition attack multi-sensor) equipped A-6Es can be distinguished by the small sensor turret located beneath the nose. These house forward looking infra-red (FLIR) and laser sensors to provide the crew with real-time television imagery of non-visual and radar transparent targets (*US Navy photo*)

Above Condensation streams from the cockpit canopy due to a combination of high speed and high humidity over the Chesapeake test range. A cluster of Mk 82 Snakeye retarded bombs fall cleanly away from one of Strike's A-6E TRAM Intruders. A total of no less than 30 Mk 82 Snakeye 500 lb bombs can be carried on the Intruder's four underwing stores pylons (*US Navy photo*)

Right Groundcrew unload flight data from the bowels of a Strike Test Directorate Grumman A-6E Intruder

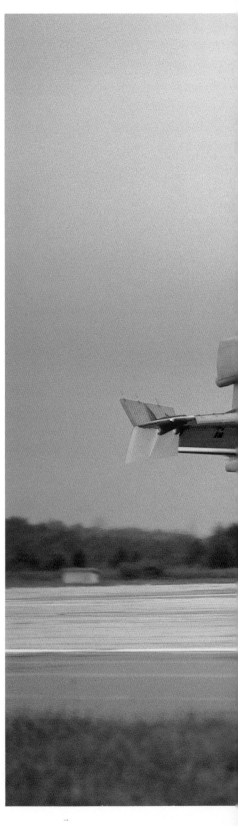

Above With the cancellation of the General Dynamics/McDonnell Douglas A-12, the US Navy is planning to upgrade an increased number of its A-6Es in order to maintain the combat capability of its attack units

Right With wing-tip airbrakes deployed, a Grumman EA-6B Prowler lands during a seasonal rain storm. Operated by Strike, this Prowler is carrying a pair of Texas Instruments AGM-88A HARM (High Speed Anti-Radiation Missiles)

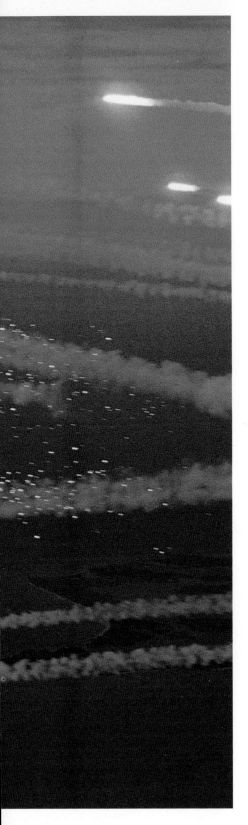

Above left Crew of a Strike A-6E have a flightline de-brief, following a weapons dispersion sortie

Above right The pilot of a Strike A-6E inspects one of the many aircraft-mounted cameras fitted for filming weapon trajectories during dispersion trials

Left A Marine Corps night-attack McDonnell Douglas AV-8B dispenses a salvo of infra-red (IR) flares. By emulating the IR characteristics of their 'parent' aircraft, flares decoy, or confuse, IR missile systems such as man-portable surface to air missiles (*US Navy photo*)

Above A heavily laden and instrumented AV-8B Harrier II climbs out from Pax River for a weapon release trial

Above right One of the projects being carried out by Strike is an engine upgrade assessment for the Harrier II, with particular consideration for shipborne operations

Right Groundcrew prepare to tow a US Marine Corps night-attack variant of the AV-8B to the Strike hangar after a test flight from Pax River. One of the less glamorous, but equally important tasks of NATC's Force directorate is the development of ground support equipment

Previous page An apparently serene in-flight refuelling by a McDonnell Douglas AV-8B Harrier II and S-3A Viking at sunset, belies the skill required to master this difficult art. The techniques required for all of the US Navy's fixed wing aircraft having an in-flight refuelling capability are developed by Strike (*US Navy photo*)

Command
and control

Eyes of the fleet, the unmistakable
silhouette of a Grumman E-2C
Hawkeye. The 24 ft diameter
rotodome houses the new total
radiation aperture control antenna
and is capable of detecting airborne
targets anywhere within a three
million cubic mile surveillance
envelope (*US Navy photo*)

Originally designed to provide advanced warning of attack by Soviet long-range bombers upon aircraft carrier battle groups, the waning of the Soviet threat is opening up new mission opportunities for the E-2C, particularly in using the aircraft to detect smaller and mobile targets ashore. An unusual view of a Force E-2C, the fairing behind the cockpit is an air-intake for the avionics system heat exchanger

Above A decal on the fuselage side of this E-2C proudly commemorates the 75th anniversary of US naval aviation, recalling the day in 1911 when the US Navy placed a requisition for two Curtiss seaplanes out of its special $25,000 budget

Right With the increasing use of tactical low-level flying to defeat ground-based radar systems, airborne early warning (AEW) aircraft are an important asset to any air arm. E-2C, BuNo 163029, is one of five Hawkeye AEW aircraft operated by Force to develop systems and tactics

Above A total of 16 EC-130Qs were built between 1967 and 1984, since when they have received a variety of systems refinements, bringing them to different standards. VQ-4's sister squadron, VQ-3, at NAS Barbers Point, Hawaii, are currently converting to the Boeing E-6 TACAMO aircraft, a variant of the commercial 707

Left Fleet Air Reconnaissance FOUR (VQ-4) is equipped with Lockheed EC-130Q TACAMO aircraft, TACAMO being an acronym for the US Marine Corps motto 'Take Charge And Move Out'. The EC-130Q has been described as the only airborne, survivable communications link with submarine forces, providing HF and VLF facilities

Above left Yet another modification to the EC-130Q fleet was the addition of a second trailing wire aerial, mounted at the rear of the fuselage under the tailplane. This supplements the deployable wire aerial of over 25,000 ft in length, for VLF communications, which feeds through the aircraft's cargo ramp

Above right Security surrounding VQ-4 is by far the highest of any unit at Pax River. This is hardly surprising considering that the primary mission of VQ-4 is to provide the President of the United States with the capability of communicating with his SSBN submarine fleet at all times, even during a nuclear war

Left An example of the modifications incorporated to the EC-130Q whilst in service are the wing-tip pods, containing classified electronics. Test and evaluation of the TACAMO's systems is carried out at Pax River by the Force directorate

Above Lt Leslie 'Ace' Pease and Lt Junior Grade Robert Sunderland. 'Ace' is an airborne communications officer and works in Operations at VQ-4; Bob Sunderland is an EC-130 second pilot, who also serves as the squadron public affairs officer. About twenty per cent of VQ-4's aircrew are female

Right Pax River maintains the only electromagnetic compatibility (EMC) facility in the United States, currently capable of providing high intensity radiated field testing on jet powered aircraft. It is occupied here by a Lockheed KC-130R of VMGR-352 from El Toro, California

Testing trainers

Immaculately maintained Northrop
T-38 Talons on the Test Pilot School's
(TPS) flightline

Above The T-38 Talon is a two-seat, twin-engine, supersonic advanced trainer aircraft, used for group aircraft flight exercises and transonic flying qualities evaluation. It introduces students without fast-jet experience to the capabilities of high performance aircraft and is also used for progress check flights

Left Student and instructor of the TPS carry out their T-38 pre-flight checks prior to taxying

Right Since this photograph of the two full-scale development McDonnell Douglas/British Aerospace T-45A Goshawks was taken in October 1990, a third aircraft, the first production Goshawk, has joined the flight test programme. The Goshawk has been chosen as a successor to the US Navy's intermediate trainer, the Rockwell International T-2C Buckeye, and will provide an integrated training system (T-4TS) for the US Navy jet trainer programme

Above The second T-45A development aircraft, BuNo 162788, landing after an evaluation sortie. Development flying is shared between Strike and the aicraft contractor company test pilots at Pax River. This 'principle site' testing concept saves considerable duplication of effort and resources. On the F-14D programme, for example, principle site testing saved approximately $50 million

Overleaf Five significant modification packages are being incorporated to the Goshawk in order to achieve the demanding handling characteristics necessary for carrier operations. These include the incorporation of a half-span wing leading-edge slat to increase the maximum lift coefficient, a configuration tested on the first development aircraft, BuNo 162787

2787

NAVY

T-45A
162787

DANGER
ARRESTING HOOK

Left Front cockpit of the second T-45A development aircraft

Right The mission of the Beechcraft T-34C is to provide primary training for the US Naval Training Command. By mid-1987 the Navy's T-34C fleet had logged over one million flying hours and had established the lowest accident rate for aircraft in the service's current inventory. The three aircraft operated by Force are used for air-to-air photography, flight test chase and to demonstrate single-engine aircraft handling qualities

Above Hand signals being used by the groundcrewman to indicate to the pilot that the T-2C's flaps are lowered

Left Blue smoke marks the touch-down point of this Rockwell International T-2C Buckeye. This two-seat, twin-engine intermediate trainer is operated by the TPS for flying qualities and performance flight exercises, night and instrument proficiency flying and progress check flights. The Buckeye also introduces students to flight at high angles of attack, and serves as the 'out of control' flight training aircraft

A total of 231 T-2Cs have been delivered to the US Naval Air Training Command for intermediate level pilot training. The tandem cockpit arrangement features a raised aft seat for improved visibility

The Bell OH-58 Kiowa is a lightweight, single engine, observation/training helicopter, used by the TPS to demonstrate a variety of rotary wing exercises, including autorotation entry and landing. It also introduces fixed wing students to VTOL flight

Above Refuelling the TPS North American SNJ-5C

Left The North American SNJ-5C bridges the generation gap as students of the TPS evaluate the aircraft in which some of their fathers were taught to fly

Pax specials

Left Initial in-flight refuelling trials of the F/A-18 Hornet were supported by the Force directorate's Convair UC-880, this unique aircraft later operating in support of the first test firings of the General Dynamics BGM-109 Tomahawk cruise missile (*US Navy photo*)

Above The performance and size/payload capacity of the UC-880 enable it to perform multiple range support functions simultaneously for extended periods and over a wide area. It is also equipped with a global positioning system, making it admirably suited for surveillance, command and control and relay tasks

Above Asymmetric power flying qualities, multi-engine performance and flying quality assessment are demonstrated by the TPS Beechcraft U-21A Ute. The Ute is also the primary fixed wing aircraft flown by the rotary wing students for turboprop familiarization and to retain currency

Left This de Havilland U-6A Beaver, BuNo 164525, is the last of its type in US Navy service. It is flown by the TPS as a back-up STOL demonstrator for the School's de Havilland Canada NU-1B Otter, and as a tow aircraft for the Schweizer X-26A sailplanes

Overleaf One of the functions of the TPS is to provide students with the opportunity of evaluating a wide variety of aircraft types and hence enable him, or her, to assess the acceptability of its flight characteristics. Paradoxically, by only flying aircraft that have already had their bugs 'ironed out', students are not exposed to unstable, inherently dangerous prototypes. Thus, in order to provide a safe demonstration of a range of handling qualities in flight, the school leases a variable-stability Gates Learjet 24, from Arvin Calspan

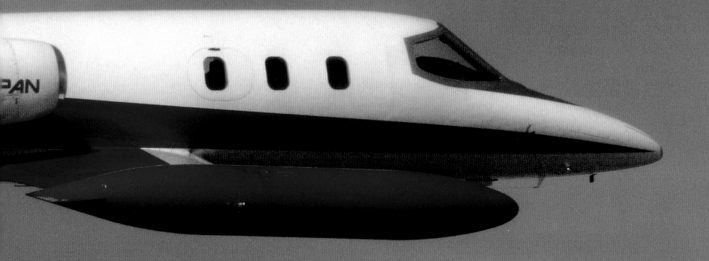

Above Maryland State Police Bell 206B JetRanger III on the TPS rotary wing flightline

Right US Coast Guard aviation is tasked with a wide range of humanitarian roles from flying intensive air operations in support of the war on drugs to search and rescue operations. It also has a defence readiness role, the US Coast Guard operating as a service within the US Navy upon declaration of war and in time of tension. There are currently some 80 fixed wing aircraft and 138 helicopters in the US Coast Guard inventory, plus several unmanned airships (aerostats). These Aerospatiale HH-65A Dolphins are on loan to the TPS from the US Coast Guard

Above Aircraft and aircrewmembers of HC-6 are frequent visitors to Pax River for logistics and passenger transfers

Left Old and new colour schemes are displayed by this pair of Boeing Vertol CH-46D Sea Knights, of Helicopter Support Squadron SIX (HC-6), based in Norfolk, Virginia

Above At the time this photograph was taken of the fourth V-22 Osprey built, in Summer 1990, the flight test programme was proceeding extremely smoothly. Perhaps that should have been a warning of the trauma to come as aircraft development is seldom painless. At the time of writing, the fifth prototype had been destroyed during take-off and funding for advanced procurement and research and development was still awaited (*US Navy photo*)

Left Improvements to the Navy's CH-46D fleet will extend their effective service life until the end of this century, at significantly reduced operating costs

Ground support

Government surplus Sgt York DIVAD (Division Air Defence) systems are used by the TPS as inexpensive teaching aids for demonstrating fire control weapon system integration. The Sgt York's Westinghouse AN/APG-66 fire control radar, developed for the General Dynamics F-16, presents target data in the form of target identity, priorities and battle status information

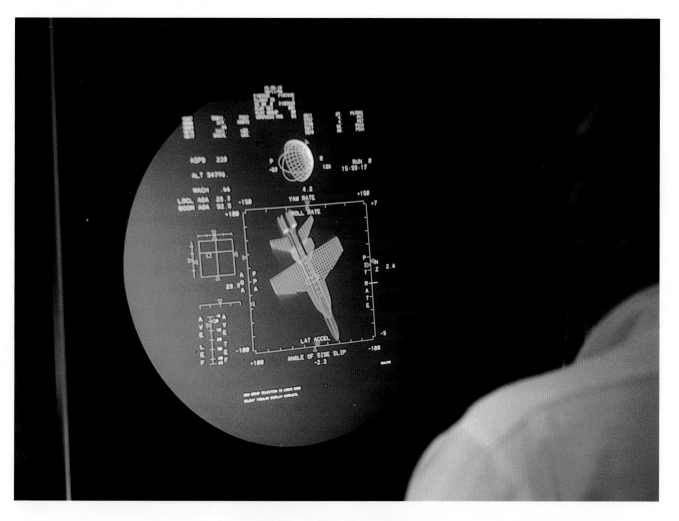

Above A broad variety of computer application programmes and output formats necessary to conduct test programmes are available to the engineer at this project engineer's station. This computer generated 3-D graphic display of an F/A-18, based on real-time performance data, is a typical example

Left A corner of the Range Directorate Telemetry Data Center, showing a section of the extensive display capabilities. They include large screen, multi-colour, interactive and 3-D displays. Information presented consist of maps, plots, graphs, out-of-limits parameters, tabular data and computer generated images that enable the range personnel to safely control and monitor multiple projects, simultaneously. The Bell/Boeing V-22 displayed in the top right of the photograph was specifically chosen for the Author's visit as the range staff had been told he was from Osprey Publishing

Flight tests from Pax River are flown over the Chesapeake Test range, an area of over 500 square miles of airspace controlled by the Naval Air Test Center. This has the advantage of short transit flight times and excellent noise abatement. These three I-Band tracking radars are part of an extensive suite of electronic and electro-optical sensor and tracking systems which provide total coverage of the Chesapeake range. For offshore flight testing over the Atlantic Ocean, the Range directorate deploys a number of support personnel to NASA Wallops

Above Plaque erected prominently beside the terminal building, in memory of Vice Admiral Frederick Mackay Trapnell, second commander of the Naval Air Test Center

Left The rural setting belies the sophistication of the GTE Pennsylvania portable laser tracker in the background. Used primarily for measuring take-off and landing performance and helicopter demonstrations, including 'hard' landings, this tracker has a range accuracy of 1 in 30,000. To aid tracking, test aircraft carry three 1 inch corner reflectors

Overleaf Control tower and arrival terminal building. Air Traffic control officers at Pax River are responsible for 7000 square miles of airspace and handle some 250,000 movements per year. Within its area of responsibility is the Chesapeake Bay restricted control zone, for supersonic runs and weapon firing/drops. The tower also monitors approaches to the airfield's automatic carrier landing system, handing over to Naval Electronic System Engineering Activity personnel for final talk-down